SECRETS OF BRINGING

Peace

ON EARTH

J. Donald Walters

Hardbound edition, first printing 1993

Copyright 1993
J. Donald Walters

Illustrations copyright 1993
Crystal Clarity, Publishers

ISBN 1-56589-050-7

10 9 8 7 6 5 4 3 2 1

PRINTED IN SINGAPORE

Crystal 🐦 *Clarity*
P U B L I S H E R S

14618 Tyler Foote Road, Nevada City, CA 95959
1 (800) 424-1055

A seed thought is offered for every day of the month. Begin a day at the appropriate date. Repeat the saying several times: first out loud, then softly, then in a whisper, and then only mentally. With each repetition, allow the words to become absorbed ever more deeply into your subconscious. Thus, gradually, you will acquire as complete an understanding as one might gain from a year's course in the subject. At this point, indeed, the truths set forth here will have become your own.

Keep the book open at the pertinent page throughout the day. Refer to it occasionally during moments of leisure. Relate the saying as often as possible to real situations in your life.

Then at night, before you go to bed, repeat the thought several times more. While falling asleep, carry the words into your subconscious, absorbing their positive influence into your whole being. Let it become thereby an integral part of your normal consciousness.

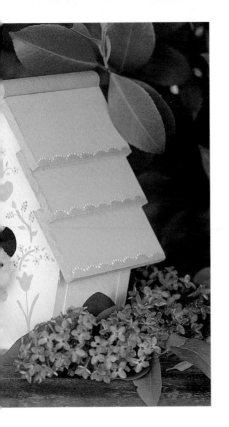

Day One

—

The secret
of bringing
Peace on
Earth is...

to remember

that whatever

peace you bring

must begin

on that little

piece of earth

where *you* live.

Day Two

—

The secret of bringing
Peace on Earth is...

first, to calm

the feelings in

your own heart.

—

Day Three

—

The secret of
bringing Peace
on Earth is...

to emanate

consciously,

from your heart,

rays of peace

into the world

around you.

Day Four

—

The secret of bringing Peace on Earth is...

to surround yourself,

wherever you go, with an aura

of peacefulness. Walk consciously

in that light of peace.

—

Day Five

—

The secret of bringing Peace on Earth is...

to touch others daily
with the wand of
your inner peace.

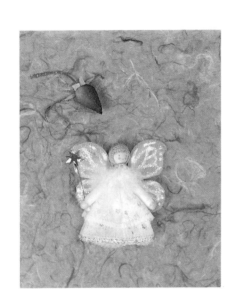

HOME
SWEET
HOME

Day Six

—

The secret of bringing
Peace on Earth is...

to live less at your

periphery, more at your

heart center.

—

Day Seven

—

The secret of bringing
Peace on Earth is...

to touch others at their center,

by reaching out to them

across a bridge of light

from your own heart.

Day Eight

—

The secret of bringing Peace on Earth is...

to think *peace* when you look
into people's eyes.

Day Nine

—

The secret of bringing Peace on Earth is...

to send *peace* into the world

by consciously projecting

a calming influence

through your voice.

—

Day Ten

—

The secret of bringing
Peace on Earth is...

to let your every movement

be an expression

of your inner peace

and harmony.

Day Eleven

—

The secret of bringing Peace on Earth is...

to realize that peace,

when you express it,

has its source

not in you—but in Infinity.

Day Twelve
—

The secret of bringing Peace on Earth is...

to understand that true

peace is never passive;

that like nourishing rain,

it sustains whatever

life it touches.

Day Thirteen

—

The secret of bringing Peace on Earth is...

seeking, wherever possible,

points of discussion on

which you and others

can agree.

Day Fourteen

—

The secret of bringing
Peace on Earth is...

never trying to make peace
at the cost of true and
noble principles.

Day Fifteen

—

The secret of bringing Peace on Earth is...

never placing expediency
above truth.

—

Day Sixteen

—

The secret of bringing Peace on Earth is...

understanding that love

is the highest truth,

the highest principle.

—

Day Seventeen

—

The secret of bringing Peace on Earth is...

to light a candle of kindness in your heart

when you feel a need to correct someone;

then, as you speak, to hold

it there unwaveringly.

Day Eighteen

—

The secret of bringing Peace on Earth is...

forgiving any who have
ever wronged you. Indeed if
you cannot offer peace to
them, how will you offer it
to others whose lives have
never touched yours?

Day Nineteen

—

The secret of bringing Peace on Earth is...

not demanding that others

live as you believe they should,

but living unassumingly

by your own beliefs.

Day Twenty

—

The secret of bringing Peace on Earth is...

bearing in mind that the world *is*,
simply, what it is. And is it so small
a place, that you could change it
radically? Live at peace with
yourself, if you would bring peace
even to one other human being.

Day Twenty-One

—

The secret of bringing Peace on Earth is...

recalling that the promise of

peace came down to earth

from heavenly regions. It is

not the gift of governments.

—

Day Twenty-Two

—

The secret of bringing
Peace on Earth is...

reflecting that peace

comes not from outer,

but from inner, victories.

Day Twenty-Three

—

The secret of bringing
Peace on Earth is...

reflecting that one single

peace-inspired, peace-inspiring thought

holds more power for peace than a

thousand shouted slogans.

—

Day Twenty-Four

—

The secret of bringing Peace on Earth is...

to place a higher priority
on holding peace in your
heart than on doing all
those little things that daily
cry out for attention.

—

The secret of bringing

on Earth is...

to accept that creating peace

is not others' job, only:

It is *your* responsibility.

—

Day Twenty-Five

—

Day Twenty-Six

—

The secret of bringing
Peace on Earth is...

not waiting for the future to bring you peace,

but living peacefully this moment,

then extending that peacefulness

from day to day into the future.

—

Day Twenty-Seven

The secret of bringing Peace on Earth is...

to live this day

well and nobly,

with kind thoughts

toward all.

Day Twenty-Eight

—

The secret of bringing Peace on Earth is...

to relinquish selfish desires,
and thereby to establish
peace and freedom
in your own heart.

—

Day Twenty-Nine

—

The secret of
bringing Peace
on Earth is...

to place more faith

in the Divine Law

than in human laws.

—

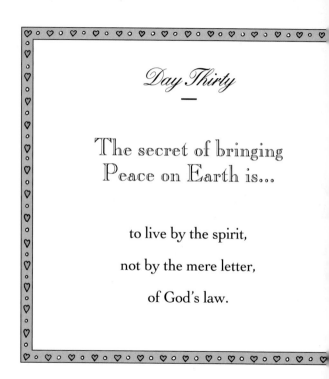

Day Thirty

—

The secret of bringing
Peace on Earth is...

to live by the spirit,

not by the mere letter,

of God's law.

Day Thirty-One

—

The secret of bringing Peace on Earth is...

to pray daily for world peace —

not as an end to strife and discord, merely,

but as the dawn of Divine Love on earth.

—

Other Books in the **Secrets** Series
by J. Donald Walters

Secrets of Happiness

Secrets of Friendship

Secrets of Love

Secrets of Inner Peace

Secrets of Success

Secrets for Men

Secrets for Women

Secrets of Prosperity

Secrets of Leadership

Secrets of Winning People

Secrets of Radiant Health and Well-Being

Secrets of Self-Acceptance